Contents

21st Century

1) Tottenham faced West Ham in Jose Mourinho's first game in charge in November 2019, what was the score?

2) In what year did Tottenham first finish above Arsenal in the Premier League in the 21st century?

3) Tottenham were denied victory against Manchester United in January 2005 after Pedro Mendes long range effort was adjudged not to have crossed the line, who was the goalkeeper who spilled his strike?

4) In what year did Teddy Sheringham re-join the club from Manchester United?

5) Who scored the final ever league goal at White Hart Lane?

6) Spurs played their first game at the Tottenham Hotspur Stadium against Crystal Palace in April 2019, what was the score?

7) Who scored the first Premier League goal at the Tottenham Hotspur Stadium?

8) Gareth Bale scored an unfortunate own goal with his face after an Aaron Lennon clearance hit off him in a game versus which team in November 2012?

9) Who scored an own goal against Chelsea in February 2019 as Tottenham went down to a 2-0 defeat at Stamford Bridge?

10) In what year did Daniel Levy become chairman of the club?

11) Spurs narrowly missed out on a Champions League place in 2006 after the squad suffered from a bout of food poisoning before their crucial match against which team on the last day of the season?

12) How old was Brad Friedel when he made his final appearance for the club?

13) What has been the clubs highest league finish this century so far?

14) What has been the clubs lowest league finish this century so far?

15) Who became the clubs youngest ever player when he made his debut against Dinamo Zagreb aged 16 years and 295 days in 2008?

16) In what year did Sol Campbell make his infamous move from Tottenham to Arsenal?

17) What was the result in Tim Sherwood's final game as Tottenham manager versus Aston Villa in May 2014?

18) Ledley King made his final Spurs appearance before retiring against which team in April 2012?

19) Who did Hugo Lloris replace as permanent club captain in August 2015?

20) Fulham beat Spurs 1-0 at White Hart Lane in March 2013, which former Spurs player scored the goal and which former Tottenham manager was in charge of Fulham?

21) In what season did Harry Kane first win the Premier League golden boot award?

22) Who became the first Russian to play for Spurs after singing for the club in 2008?

23) In what seasons did Gareth Bale win the PFA player of the year award?

24) Which Spurs defender won the PFA young player of the year award in 2011/12?

Transfers I

1) Which goalkeeper was signed on a free from Wimbledon in May 2000?

2) Which striker was signed for £11 million from Dynamo Kiev in June 2000?

3) David Ginola left the club in 2000 to join which team?

4) Which midfielder was signed from Chelsea in June 2001?

5) Defender Christian Ziege was bought from which English club in 2001?

6) Long-serving goalkeeper Ian Walker left to join which team in 2001?

7) Striker Robbie Keane was bought from where in 2002?

8) Tim Sherwood left Spurs in January 2003 to sign for which team?

9) Which striker was signed from Porto in 2003?

10) Which central midfielder left the club in 2003 to join Kaiserslautern?

11) Jermain Defoe was bought from which club in February 2004?

12) Who did Sergei Rebrov sign for after leaving Spurs in 2004?

13) Which club did Jamie Redknapp sign for from Tottenham in January 2005?

14) Which two players did Tottenham sign from Nottingham Forest in January 2005?

15) Which young winger was bought from Leeds United in 2005?

First Goals I – Name the clubs that these players scored their first goal for Tottenham against

1) Harry Kane

2) Gareth Bale

3) Luka Modric

4) Darren Bent

5) Jermain Defoe

6) Peter Crouch

7) Robbie Keane

8) Freddie Kanoute

9) Ledley King

10) Aaron Lennon

11) Son Heung-Min

12) Dele Alli

Red Cards

1) Which two Spurs players were sent off during their 1-0 defeat away to Bournemouth in May 2019?

2) Son Heung-Min was sent off against Everton in 2019 for a challenge which resulted in which opposition player suffering an horrendous ankle injury?

3) Which player received two red cards in one week by being dismissed against Manchester United and Chelsea in 2002?

4) Which Tottenham defender was dismissed in the late stages of the 4-2 defeat to Arsenal in December 2018?

5) Goalkeeper Hugo Lloris saw red in a Champions League match against which club in October 2018?

6) Which Tottenham player was sent off against him former club in the 5-2 North London derby defeat versus Arsenal in November 2012?

7) Tottenham had also lost 5-2 against Arsenal in the February of 2012, which Spurs player was dismissed on that occasion?

8) Which midfielder was sent off during the 1-1 draw with Arsenal in April 2006, the last North London derby played at Highbury?

9) Which two Spurs players were sent off during the 2-1 defeat against Stoke in October 2008, the final match with Juande Ramos as Tottenham manager?

10) Who was sent off against Everton in August 2001, only to have the decision rescinded on appeal?

11) Which midfielder saw red against Norwich in a 1-1 draw in September 2012, later having the decision overturned?

Memorable Goals

1) Who scored the Premier League goal of the season for 2015/16 with his volley versus Crystal Palace?

2) Which player scored a stunning left footed volley on his league debut versus Arsenal in April 2010?

3) Gareth Bale scored the goal of the month for August 2010 with his exquisite volley against which team?

4) Gareth Bale ran more than half the length of the pitch before producing a clinical finish with the outside of his boot against which team in January 2013?

5) Which defender struck a spectacular long-range goal against Liverpool at Anfield in April 2005?

6) Paul Robinson scored past which fellow goalkeeper in the 3-1 win over Watford in 2007?

7) Which unexpected player crashed in power equaliser from outside the box against Liverpool in February 2018?

8) Who registered a goal against Bradford City after just 10 seconds of their game in December 2000?

9) Son Heung-Min produced a spectacular solo run and finish to score one of the best individual goals in Premier League history against which team in December 2019?

10) Who scored the Premier League goal of the month with his long-range volley in the 4-4 draw with Arsenal in October 2008?

11) Who scored on his debut in a 2-0 win over Manchester City in February 2020?

12) Who did Harry Kane score his 100th Premier League goal against in 2018?

13) Robbie Keane scored an unusual goal against Birmingham in 2003 by waiting behind the goalkeeper and waiting for him to drop the ball, before stealing it off him and rolling the ball into the empty net. Who was the goalkeeper?

Transfers II

1) Who was signed on a free from Inter Milan in August 2005?

2) Dimitar Berbatov was bought from which German club in 2006?

3) Which midfielder was sold to Manchester United in July 2006?

4) Who was bought from Southampton for a reported £7 million in May 2007?

5) Younes Kaboul arrive in 2007 from which French club?

6) Where was Luka Modric bought from in 2008?

7) Which played was signed from Barcelona in June 2008?

8) Robbie Keane was sold to which club in July 2008?

9) Tottenham signed which goalkeeper on a free from Chelsea in January 2009?

10) Who were the two players signed from Sheffield United in July 2009?

11) Darren Bent was sold to which club in 2009?

12) Who arrived from Real Madrid in August 2010?

13) Goalkeeper Brad Friedel signed from which team in July 2011?

14) Robbie Keane was sold to which club in August 2011?

15) Which centre back was bought from Ajax in 2012?

Memorable Games

1) What was the final score as Tottenham and Chelsea produced a classic encounter in January 2015 at White Hart Lane?

2) Spurs were leading 3-0 at home at half time against Manchester United in September 2001, what was the final score?

3) Spurs qualified for the Champions League by beating Manchester City 1-0 away from home in May 2010, who grabbed the only goal of the game?

4) Who scored a hat-trick as Spurs beat Southampton 5-1 at home in December 2004?

5) Who scored the last-minute equaliser in the dramatic 4-4 draw with Arsenal in October 2008?

6) Who grabbed 4 assists and a goal for himself in the 5-0 demolishing of Newcastle in February 2012?

7) Who did Tottenham draw 2-2 with in May 2016 to hand the Premier League title to Leicester City?

8) Which player scored 5 goals in the 9-1 hammering of Wigan in November 2009?

9) Which team did Spurs beat 7-1 away from home in May 2017?

10) Who was in goal as Tottenham were hammered 6-0 away to Manchester City in November 2013?

11) Robbie Keane scored a hat-trick in a 4-3 win over which club in January 2003?

First Goals II

1) Michael Carrick
2) Jan Vertonghen
3) Gus Poyet
4) Sergei Rebrov
5) Roberto Soldado
6) Simon Davies
7) Danny Murphy
8) Jamie O'Hara
9) Dimitar Berbatov
10) Mido
11) Roman Pavlyuchenko
12) Vincent Janssen

Cup Games

1) Tottenham hammered Arsenal over two legs in the semi-final of the 2008 League Cup, what was the final score on aggregate?

2) Who scored the winner in extra time as Spurs beat Chelsea in the League Cup final of 2008?

3) Who scored Tottenham's goal as they lost 2-1 to Blackburn in the League Cup final in 2002?

4) Tottenham went down to a 4-1 defeat on penalties against Manchester United in the 2009 League Cup final, who was the only Spurs player to score his penalty in the shoot-out?

5) Spurs lost the 2015 League Cup final 2-0 to Chelsea, which Tottenham player scored an own goal in the match?

6) Which lower league side knocked Tottenham out of the League Cup in September 2019?

7) Tottenham beat Liverpool 4-2 in the League Cup 4th round in 2008, which two players grabbed braces for Spurs?

8) Which lower league team beat Spurs in the second round of the League Cup in 2005?

9) Spurs collapsed to a 4-3 defeat, after leading 3-0 at half-time against which team in the FA Cup 4th round in 2004?

10) Which player scored the winner as Leicester beat Spurs 3-2 in the FA Cup in 2005?

11) Spurs hammered which lower league side 7-0 away from home in the FA Cup 3rd round of 2019?

12) Tottenham were 3-2 going into the last minute of their 3rd round FA Cup tie in 2017 before scoring twice to win 4-3 against which club?

Transfers III

1) Goalkeeper Hugo Lloris was bought from which French club in 2012?

2) Luka Modric was sold to which club in 2012?

3) Who arrived from Roma in August 2013?

4) Heurelho Gomes left Spurs in 2014 and signed for which team?

5) From which club was Eric Dier bought from in 2014?

6) Where was Dele Alli signed from in February 2015?

7) Toby Alderweireld arrived from which team in 2015?

8) Which attacking player was bought from Bayer Leverkusen in 2015?

9) Where did Roberto Soldado go to from Spurs in 2015?

10) Vincent Janssen was signed from which Dutch team in 2016?

11) From which club did Spurs sign Fernando Llorente in 2017?

12) Who was signed from PSG in January 2018?

13) Which player arrived from Fulham in August 2019?

14) Tanguy Ndombele arrived from which French side in July 2019?

European Games

1) Gareth Bale scored a sensational Champions League hat-trick away against Inter Milan in 2010, but what was the final score of the game?

2) Spurs beat AC Milan 1-0 away from home in the first leg of their 2011 Champions League tie, who scored the only goal of the game?

3) During that 2011 game, AC Milan midfielder Gennaro Gattuso infamously headbutted which member of the Tottenham coaching staff?

4) Tottenham beat Dinamo Zagreb 4-0 in the UEFA Cup in 2008, thanks in part to a hat-trick from who?

5) Erik Lamela scored with a spectacular rabona shot against which side in the Europa League in 2014?

6) Who was penalised for handball in the first minute of the 2019 Champions League final to give Liverpool a controversial penalty?

7) Who scored the last-minute winner against Ajax to dramatically send Spurs into the Champions League final in 2019?

8) Harry Kane scored a hat-trick and finished the match in goal against which team in a Europa League match in 2014?

9) Harry Kane missed a penalty on his Tottenham debut in a 2011 Europa League tie against which side?

10) Who scored a last-minute winner to knock Lyon out of the Europe League in 2013?

11) Tottenham were knocked out of the Europa League in March 2016 by Borussia Dortmund, which future Arsenal player scored three times in the tie?

12) Tottenham qualified for the 2019 Champions League semi-finals after which player scored a controversial late goal against Manchester City to send Spurs through on away goals?

21st Century – Answers

1) Tottenham faced West Ham in Jose Mourinho's first game in charge in November 2019, what was the score?
West Ham 2-3 Tottenham Hotspur

2) In what year did Tottenham first finish above Arsenal in the Premier League in the 21st century?
2017

3) Tottenham were denied victory against Manchester United in January 2005 after Pedro Mendes long range effort was adjudged not to have crossed the line, who was the goalkeeper who spilled his strike?
Roy Carroll

4) In what year did Teddy Sheringham re-join the club from Manchester United?
2001

5) Who scored the final ever league goal at White Hart Lane?
Wayne Rooney

6) Spurs played their first game at the Tottenham Hotspur Stadium against Crystal Palace in April 2019, what was the score?
Tottenham Hotspur 2-0 Crystal Palace

7) Who scored the first Premier League goal at the Tottenham Hotspur Stadium?
Son Heung-Min

8) Gareth Bale scored an unfortunate own goal with his face after an Aaron Lennon clearance hit off him in a game versus which team in November 2012?
Liverpool

9) Who scored an own goal against Chelsea in February 2019 as Tottenham went down to a 2-0 defeat at Stamford Bridge?
   Kieran Trippier

10) In what year did Daniel Levy become chairman of the club?
   2001

11) Spurs narrowly missed out on a Champions League place in 2006 after the squad suffered from a bout of food poisoning before their crucial match against which team on the last day of the season?
   West Ham

12) How old was Brad Friedel when he made his final appearance for the club?
   42

13) What has been the clubs highest league finish this century so far?
2nd in 2016/17

14) What has been the clubs lowest league finish this century so far?
14th in 2003/04

15) Who became the clubs youngest ever player when he made his debut against Dinamo Zagreb aged 16 years and 295 days in 2008?
John Bostock

16) In what year did Sol Campbell make his infamous move from Tottenham to Arsenal?
2001

17) What was the result in Tim Sherwood's final game as Tottenham manager versus Aston Villa in May 2014?
Tottenham 3-0 Aston Villa

18) Ledley King made his final Spurs appearance before retiring against which team in April 2012?
QPR

19) Who did Hugo Lloris replace as permanent club captain in August 2015?
Younes Kaboul

20) Fulham beat Spurs 1-0 at White Hart Lane in March 2013, which former Spurs player scored the goal and which former Tottenham manager was in charge of Fulham?
Dimitar Berbatov and Martin Jol

21) In what season did Harry Kane first win the Premier League golden boot award?
2015/16

22) Who became the first Russian to play for Spurs after singing for the club in 2008?
Roman Pavlyuchenko

23) In what seasons did Gareth Bale win the PFA player of the year award?
2010/11 and 2012/13

24) Which Spurs defender won the PFA young player of the year award in 2011/12?
Kyle Walker

Transfers I – Answers

1) Which goalkeeper was signed on a free from Wimbledon in May 2000?
   Neil Sullivan

2) Which striker was signed for £11 million from Dynamo Kiev in June 2000?
   Sergei Rebrov

3) David Ginola left the club in 2000 to join which team?
   Aston Villa

4) Which midfielder was signed from Chelsea in June 2001?
   Gus Poyet

5) Defender Christian Ziege was bought from which English club in 2001?
   Liverpool

6) Long-serving goalkeeper Ian Walker left to join which team in 2001?
   Leicester City

7) Striker Robbie Keane was bought from where in 2002?
Leeds United

8) Tim Sherwood left Spurs in January 2003 to sign for which team?
Portsmouth

9) Which striker was signed from Porto in 2003?
Helder Postiga

10) Which central midfielder left the club in 2003 to join Kaiserslautern?
Steffen Freund

11) Jermain Defoe was bought from which club in February 2004?
West Ham

12) Who did Sergei Rebrov sign for after leaving Spurs in 2004?
West Ham

13) Which club did Jamie Redknapp sign for from Tottenham in January 2005?
Southampton

14) Which two players did Tottenham sign from Nottingham Forest in January 2005?
Michael Dawson and Andy Reid

15) Which young winger was bought from Leeds United in 2005?
Aaron Lennon

First Goals I – Answers

1) Harry Kane
Shamrock Rovers

2) Gareth Bale
Fulham

3) Luka Modric
Spartak Moscow

4) Darren Bent
Derby County

5) Jermain Defoe
Portsmouth

6) Peter Crouch
Doncaster Rovers

7) Robbie Keane
Blackburn Rovers

8) Freddie Kanoute
Leeds United

9) Ledley King
   Bradford City

10) Aaron Lennon
   Birmingham City

11) Son Heung-Min
   Qarabag

12) Dele Alli
   Leicester City

Red Cards – Answers

1) Which two Spurs players were sent off during their 1-0 defeat away to Bournemouth in May 2019?
   Juan Foyth and Son Heung-Min

2) Son Heung-Min was sent off against Everton in 2019 for a challenge which resulted in which opposition player suffering an horrendous ankle injury?
   Andre Gomes

3) Which player received two red cards in one week by being dismissed against Manchester United and Chelsea in 2002?
   Mauricio Taricco

4) Which Tottenham defender was dismissed in the late stages of the 4-2 defeat to Arsenal in December 2018?
   Jan Vertonghen

5) Goalkeeper Hugo Lloris saw red in a Champions League match against which club in October 2018?
   PSV Eindhoven

6) Which Tottenham player was sent off against him former club in the 5-2 North London derby defeat versus Arsenal in November 2012?
   Emmanuel Adebayor

7) Tottenham had also lost 5-2 against Arsenal in the February of 2012, which Spurs player was dismissed on that occasion?
   Scott Parker

8) Which midfielder was sent off during the 1-1 draw with Arsenal in April 2006, the last North London derby played at Highbury?
   Edgar Davids

9) Which two Spurs players were sent off during the 2-1 defeat against Stoke in October 2008, the final match with Juande Ramos as Tottenham manager?
Gareth Bale and Michael Dawson

10) Who was sent off against Everton in August 2001, only to have the decision rescinded on appeal?
Gary Doherty

11) Which midfielder saw red against Norwich in a 1-1 draw in September 2012, later having the decision overturned?
Tom Huddlestone

Memorable Goals – Answers

1) Who scored the Premier League goal of the season for 2015/16 with his volley versus Crystal Palace?
   Dele Alli

2) Which player scored a stunning left footed volley on his league debut versus Arsenal in April 2010?
   Danny Rose

3) Gareth Bale scored the goal of the month for August 2010 with his exquisite volley against which team?
   Stoke City

4) Gareth Bale ran more than half the length of the pitch before producing a clinical finish with the outside of his boot against which team in January 2013?
   Norwich City

5) Which defender struck a spectacular long-range goal against Liverpool at Anfield in April 2005?
Erik Edman

6) Paul Robinson scored past which fellow goalkeeper in the 3-1 win over Watford in 2007?
Ben Foster

7) Which unexpected player crashed in power equaliser from outside the box against Liverpool in February 2018?
Victor Wanyama

8) Who registered a goal against Bradford City after just 10 seconds of their game in December 2000?
Ledley King

9) Son Heung-Min produced a spectacular solo run and finish to score one of the best individual goals in Premier League history against which team in December 2019?
Burnley

10) Who scored the Premier League goal of the month with his long-range volley in the 4-4 draw with Arsenal in October 2008?
David Bentley

11) Who scored on his debut in a 2-0 win over Manchester City in February 2020?
Steven Bergwijn

12) Who did Harry Kane score his 100th Premier League goal against in 2018?
Liverpool

13) Robbie Keane scored an unusual goal against Birmingham in 2003 by waiting behind the goalkeeper and waiting for him to drop the ball, before stealing it off him and rolling the ball into the empty net. Who was the goalkeeper?
Andy Marriott

Transfers II – Answers

1) Who was signed on a free from Inter Milan in August 2005?
   Edgar Davids

2) Dimitar Berbatov was bought from which German club in 2006?
   Bayer Leverkusen

3) Which midfielder was sold to Manchester United in July 2006?
   Michael Carrick

4) Who was bought from Southampton for a reported £7 million in May 2007?
   Gareth Bale

5) Younes Kaboul arrive in 2007 from which French club?
   Auxerre

6) Where was Luka Modric bought from in 2008?
   Dinamo Zagreb

7) Which played was signed from Barcelona in June 2008?
Giovani Dos Santos

8) Robbie Keane was sold to which club in July 2008?
Liverpool

9) Tottenham signed which goalkeeper on a free from Chelsea in January 2009?
Carlo Cudicini

10) Who were the two players signed from Sheffield United in July 2009?
Kyle Naughton and Kyle Walker

11) Darren Bent was sold to which club in 2009?
Sunderland

12) Who arrived from Real Madrid in August 2010?
Rafael van der Vaart

13) Goalkeeper Brad Friedel signed from which team in July 2011?
Aston Villa

14) Robbie Keane was sold to which club in August 2011?
LA Galaxy

15) Which centre back was bought from Ajax in 2012?
Jan Vertonghen

Memorable Games – Answers

1) What was the final score as Tottenham and Chelsea produced a classic encounter in January 2015 at White Hart Lane?
   Tottenham 5-3 Chelsea

2) Spurs were leading 3-0 at home at half time against Manchester United in September 2001, what was the final score?
   Tottenham 3-5 Man Utd

3) Spurs qualified for the Champions League by beating Manchester City 1-0 away from home in May 2010, who grabbed the only goal of the game?
   Peter Crouch

4) Who scored a hat-trick as Spurs beat Southampton 5-1 at home in December 2004?
   Jermain Defoe

5) Who scored the last-minute equaliser in the dramatic 4-4 draw with Arsenal in October 2008?
Aaron Lennon

6) Who grabbed 4 assists and a goal for himself in the 5-0 demolishing of Newcastle in February 2012?
Emmanuel Adebayor

7) Who did Tottenham draw 2-2 with in May 2016 to hand the Premier League title to Leicester City?
Chelsea

8) Which player scored 5 goals in the 9-1 hammering of Wigan in November 2009?
Jermain Defoe

9) Which team did Spurs beat 7-1 away from home in May 2017?
Hull City

10) Who was in goal as Tottenham were hammered 6-0 away to Manchester City in November 2013?
Hugo Lloris

11) Robbie Keane scored a hat-trick in a 4-3 win over which club in January 2003?
Everton

First Goals II – Answers

1) Michael Carrick
   Sunderland

2) Jan Vertonghen
   Carlisle United

3) Gus Poyet
   Tranmere Rovers

4) Sergei Rebrov
   Everton

5) Roberto Soldado
   Crystal Palace

6) Simon Davies
   Bradford City

7) Danny Murphy
   Portsmouth

8) Jamie O'Hara
   Slavia Prague

9) Dimitar Berbatov
Sheffield United

10) Mido
Portsmouth

11) Roman Pavlyuchenko
Newcastle United

12) Vincent Janssen
Gillingham

Cup Games – Answers

1) Tottenham hammered Arsenal over two legs in the semi-final of the 2008 League Cup, what was the final score on aggregate?
   6-2

2) Who scored the winner in extra time as Spurs beat Chelsea in the League Cup final of 2008?
   Jonathan Woodgate

3) Who scored Tottenham's goal as they lost 2-1 to Blackburn in the League Cup final in 2002?
   Christian Ziege

4) Tottenham went down to a 4-1 defeat on penalties against Manchester United in the 2009 League Cup final, who was the only Spurs player to score his penalty in the shoot-out?
   Vedran Corluka

5) Spurs lost the 2015 League Cup final 2-0 to Chelsea, which Tottenham player scored an own goal in the match?
Kyle Walker

6) Which lower league side knocked Tottenham out of the League Cup in September 2019?
Colchester United

7) Tottenham beat Liverpool 4-2 in the League Cup 4th round in 2008, which two players grabbed braces for Spurs?
Roman Pavlyuchenko and Fraizer Campbell

8) Which lower league team beat Spurs in the second round of the League Cup in 2005?
Grimsby Town

9) Spurs collapsed to a 4-3 defeat, after leading 3-0 at half-time against which team in the FA Cup 4th round in 2004?
Manchester City

10) Which player scored the winner as Leicester beat Spurs 3-2 in the FA Cup in 2005?
Mark de Vries

11) Spurs hammered which lower league side 7-0 away from home in the FA Cup 3rd round of 2019?
Tranmere Rovers

12) Tottenham were 3-2 going into the last minute of their 3rd round FA Cup tie in 2017 before scoring twice to win 4-3 against which club?
Wycombe Wanderers

Transfers III – Answers

1) Goalkeeper Hugo Lloris was bought from which French club in 2012?
   Lyon

2) Luka Modric was sold to which club in 2012?
   Real Madrid

3) Who arrived from Roma in August 2013?
   Erik Lamela

4) Heurelho Gomes left Spurs in 2014 and signed for which team?
   Watford

5) From which club was Eric Dier bought from in 2014?
   Sporting Lisbon

6) Where was Dele Alli signed from in February 2015?
   MK Dons

7) Toby Alderweireld arrived from which team in 2015?
Atletico Madrid

8) Which attacking player was bought from Bayer Leverkusen in 2015?
Son Heung-Min

9) Where did Roberto Soldado go to from Spurs in 2015?
Villarreal

10) Vincent Janssen was signed from which Dutch team in 2016?
AZ Alkmaar

11) From which club did Spurs sign Fernando Llorente in 2017?
Swansea City

12) Who was signed from PSG in January 2018?
Lucas Moura

13) Which player arrived from Fulham in August 2019?
Ryan Sessegnon

14) Tanguy Ndombele arrived from which French side in July 2019?
Lyon

European Games – Answers

1) Gareth Bale scored a sensational Champions League hat-trick away against Inter Milan in 2010, but what was the final score of the game?
   Inter Milan 4-3 Tottenham Hotspur

2) Spurs beat AC Milan 1-0 away from home in the first leg of their 2011 Champions League tie, who scored the only goal of the game?
   Peter Crouch

3) During that 2011 game, AC Milan midfielder Gennaro Gattuso infamously headbutted which member of the Tottenham coaching staff?
   Joe Jordan

4) Tottenham beat Dinamo Zagreb 4-0 in the UEFA Cup in 2008, thanks in part to a hat-trick from who?
   Darren Bent

5) Erik Lamela scored with a spectacular rabona shot against which side in the Europa League in 2014?
   Asteras Tripolis

6) Who was penalised for handball in the first minute of the 2019 Champions League final to give Liverpool a controversial penalty?
   Moussa Sissoko

7) Who scored the last-minute winner against Ajax to dramatically send Spurs into the Champions League final in 2019?
   Lucas Moura

8) Harry Kane scored a hat-trick and finished the match in goal against which team in a Europa League match in 2014?
   Asteras Tripolis

9) Harry Kane missed a penalty on his Tottenham debut in a 2011 Europa League tie against which side?
Hearts

10) Who scored a last-minute winner to knock Lyon out of the Europe League in 2013?
Mousa Dembele

11) Tottenham were knocked out of the Europa League in March 2016 by Borussia Dortmund, which future Arsenal player scored three times in the tie?
Pierre-Emerick Aubameyang

12) Tottenham qualified for the 2019 Champions League semi-finals after which player scored a controversial late goal against Manchester City to send Spurs through on away goals?
Fernando Llorente

Printed by Amazon Italia Logistica S.r.l.
Torrazza Piemonte (TO), Italy

15973816R00039